Date: 7/17/12

LET'S ROCK

METAMORPHIC ROCKS

CHRIS OXLADE

Heinemann
LIBRARY

Chicago, Illinois

www.heinemannraintree.com
Visit our website to find out more information about Heinemann-Raintree books.

To order:
☎ Phone 888-454-2279
💻 Visit www.heinemannraintree.com to browse our catalog and order online.

Edited by Louise Galpine and Diyan Leake
Designed by Victoria Allen
Illustrated by KJA artists
Picture research by Hannah Taylor
Originated by Capstone Global Library Ltd
Printed in the United States of America by Worzalla Publishing

062011
006232RP

Library of Congress Cataloging-in-Publication Data
Oxlade, Chris.
  Metamorphic rocks / Chris Oxlade.
    p. cm. — (Let's rock!)
  Includes bibliographical references and index.
  ISBN 978-1-4329-4680-7 (hb)
  ISBN 978-1-4329-4688-3 (pb)
  1. Rocks, Metamorphic—Juvenile literature. 2. Petrology—Juvenile literature. I. Title.
  QE475.A2O95 2011
  552'.4—dc22   2010022203

Acknowledgments
The author and publisher are grateful to the following for permission to reproduce copyright material: Alamy Images pp. **4** (© Linda Reinink-Smith), **14** (© Lynne Evans), **16** (© Dennis Cox), **18** (© Antony Ratcliffe), **24** (© Toby Adamson); © Capstone Publishers p. **29** (Karon Dubke); Corbis pp. **12** (Visuals Unlimited), **19** (Lee Frost/Robert Harding World Imagery); GeoScience Features Picture Library p. **10** left and right (Prof. B Booth); reproduced with the permission of Natural Resources Canada 2010, courtesy of the Geological Survey of Canada p. **15**; Photolibrary pp. **17** (Rob Jung), **20** (Superstock), **21** (Jeffery Titcomb), **22** (Robert Harding/Roy Rainford), **23** (Joe Cornish), **26** (Britain on View/Steve Lewis); Science Photo Library pp. **5** (Gregory Dimijian), **9** (G. Brad Lewis), **11** (Dirk Wiersma).

Cover photograph of mountain peaks in the Mont Blanc range of the French Alps reproduced with permission of Photolibrary (Robert Harding Travel/Peter Richardson).

We would like to thank Dr. Stuart Robinson for his invaluable help in the preparation of this book.

Every effort has been made to contact copyright holders of any material reproduced in this book. Any omissions will be rectified in subsequent printings if notice is given to the publisher.

Disclaimer
All the Internet addresses (URLs) given in this book were valid at the time of going to press. However, due to the dynamic nature of the Internet, some addresses may have changed, or sites may have changed or ceased to exist since publication. While the author and publisher regret any inconvenience this may cause readers, no responsibility for any such changes can be accepted by either the author or the publisher.

CONTENTS

Rock roles

Find out about the work involved in the study of rocks.

Science tip

Check out our smart tips to learn more about rocks.

Number crunching

Discover the amazing numbers in the world of rocks.

Biography

Read about people who have made important discoveries in the study of rocks.

Some words are printed in bold, **like this**. You can find out what they mean by looking in the glossary on page 30.

WHAT ARE METAMORPHIC ROCKS?

Down inside Earth, many miles below the surface, hot **molten** rock forces its way upward through cracks in the solid rock nearer the surface. Heat from the molten rock flows into the solid rock, heating that rock to temperatures of hundreds of degrees—and even over a thousand degrees—Fahrenheit. The heat makes it change into a new type of rock, called metamorphic rock. The word *metamorphic* means "changing form."

MINERALS AND CRYSTALS

All rock, not just metamorphic rock, is made from materials called **minerals**. Metamorphic rocks are made from a mixture of different minerals, and sometimes just one mineral. Minerals themselves are made up of **atoms**, which are arranged in rows and columns. Materials with atoms arranged like this are called **crystals**.

This is an outcrop of **gneiss** (say "nice"), a common metamorphic rock, on the west coast of Sweden.

This is a sample of a mineral called labradorite, which is found in some metamorphic rocks. It comes in several colors, not just blue.

THREE TYPES OF ROCK

Metamorphic rock is just one type of rock. The other two types are **sedimentary rock** and **igneous rock**. Sedimentary rock is made when tiny pieces of rock, or the skeletons or shells of sea animals, are buried underground and compressed. Igneous rock is made when molten rock cools and becomes solid.

THE ROCK CYCLE

New metamorphic rock is always being formed, and it is always being destroyed. This is part of a process called the **rock cycle**. In this book we follow the journey of metamorphic rock as it moves around the rock cycle. You can see a diagram of the rock cycle on page 8.

WHAT IS INSIDE EARTH?

Earth is a giant ball of rock. If you dig a hole deep enough anywhere on Earth, you will eventually come to solid rock. This is part of the rocky outer layer that covers Earth, called the **crust**. Some of the rock is metamorphic rock. Most metamorphic rocks begin their journey inside the crust.

HOW THICK IS THE CRUST?

Under the **continents** the crust is between 25 and 90 kilometers (15 and 56 miles) thick, but under the oceans it is only between 6 and 11 kilometers (4 and 7 miles) thick. The crust sits on top of very hot rock below. This hot rock forms a layer 2,900 kilometers (1,800 miles) deep called the **mantle**.

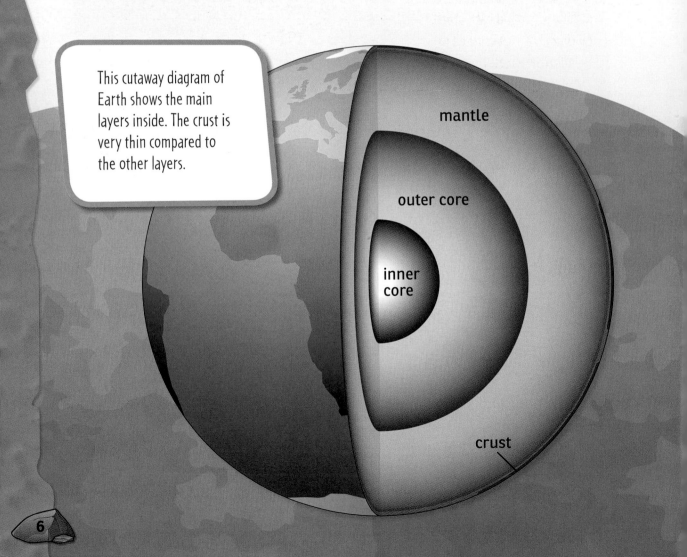

This cutaway diagram of Earth shows the main layers inside. The crust is very thin compared to the other layers.

mantle

outer core

inner core

crust

A CRACKED CRUST

The crust is cracked into many large pieces called **tectonic plates**. They move around, but only at speeds of a few inches a year. The lines where the plates meet each other are called **plate boundaries**. At some boundaries the plates move toward each other, and here rocks are destroyed and changed.

Number crunching

Many metamorphic rocks are produced by immense heat in the crust or in **magma**. At the bottom of the crust the temperature of the rocks is about 900 °C (1,652 °F). Magma can be hotter, up to 1,300 °C (2,372 °F). The heat comes from inside Earth. The temperature in Earth's **core** is about 5,500 °C (9,932 °F).

Here, two tectonic plates are moving toward each other. Their rocks are crushed by immense forces. Metamorphic rocks are often formed here.

metamorphic rocks formed here

crust

mantle

plates moving toward each other

THE ROCK CYCLE

During the **rock cycle**, new rocks, including metamorphic rocks, are made all the time, and old rocks are destroyed all the time. Most metamorphic rocks are made from **sedimentary rocks** and **igneous rocks**. You can find out how sedimentary and igneous rocks are changed into metamorphic rocks on page 10.

The change that happens when a rock becomes a metamorphic rock is called **metamorphism**. Most metamorphic rock takes thousands or millions of years to form, but it can take billions of years to move through the crust before finally being destroyed.

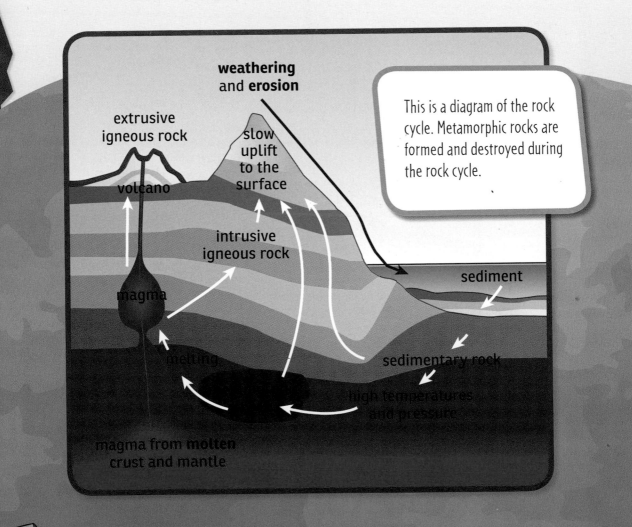

weathering and erosion

extrusive igneous rock

slow uplift to the surface

volcano

intrusive igneous rock

magma

melting

magma from **molten** crust and mantle

sediment

sedimentary rock

high temperatures and pressure

This is a diagram of the rock cycle. Metamorphic rocks are formed and destroyed during the rock cycle.

CHANGING BACK

In the rock cycle, metamorphic rocks and other rocks are also **recycled** into new rocks, which may be sedimentary or igneous rocks. Some sedimentary rocks, such as sandstone and clay, are made from **particles** (very small pieces) of other rocks joined together. Some igneous rocks are made when other rocks melt and then cool again.

Biography

Charles Lyell (1797–1875) was a Scottish scientist who traveled long distances to study rock formations in Europe, including the volcano Mount Etna in Sicily. Through his observations, he realized that Earth's surface is changing all the time. He concluded that the mountains, valleys, and other features on Earth's surface are made naturally over millions of years. At that time, most people thought that Earth was just a few thousand years old.

This is a lava flow from Kilauea, a volcano on the island of Hawaii. Some of the **minerals** in this rock may have come from metamorphic rock that has melted.

HOW ARE METAMORPHIC ROCKS MADE?

The journey of metamorphic rocks begins with other types of rock. They can be **igneous rocks**, **sedimentary rocks**, or even other metamorphic rocks. The rocks change to metamorphic rocks when they are heated, or put under immense **pressure**, or both. The rocks do not melt, but their **minerals** are destroyed and **crystals** of new minerals form. Nothing is added to the rocks as they change, and nothing is taken away. The chemicals that make up the minerals are just rearranged to make new minerals.

Shale (left) is a sedimentary rock. Under immense heat and pressure, it can become gneiss (right), a metamorphic rock.

WHERE METAMORPHIC ROCKS COME FROM

So, where are the conditions right for metamorphic rocks to be made? The answer is where there is either **magma** to provide heat, or where there is great pressure in the **crust**. Magma is produced at **destructive boundaries**, and great pressure is created in the crust at **collision boundaries**, so these are the places where most metamorphic rocks are made.

Science tip

When metamorphic rocks are made, the crystals of minerals in the rock are changed. You can see crystals of minerals in some types of rock. Look at them close up with a magnifying glass. You can easily see crystals in metamorphic rocks called **schists** and **gneisses**. Or you can examine **granite**, a common igneous rock.

This photo shows a band of speckled white, black, and blue **quartz** surrounded by slate.

METAMORPHIC ROCKS MADE BY HEAT

Some metamorphic rocks begin their journey when rocks are touched by red-hot magma in the crust. Only those rocks that are close enough to the magma to be heated will be changed. Rocks far from the magma are not changed at all. This sort of change is called **local metamorphism**. (It is also called contact metamorphism.)

Local metamorphism happens wherever magma rises into the crust. The magma might be on its way to the surface to form a **volcano**, or rising into the rocks above to form a huge bulge of new igneous rock. The bulge is called an intrusion.

When red-hot lava like this flows over existing rock, the rock may be changed by the immense heat.

HOW HEAT CHANGES ROCKS

Magma is hot—extremely hot! It can have a temperature of 1,000 °C (1,832 °F) or more. It heats up any solid rock it touches. The rocks it touches are cooked, and their minerals change. Imagine magma flowing next to mudstone, which is a sedimentary rock. Because of the heat, new minerals form in the mudstone, creating a metamorphic rock with dark spots in it called hornfels.

Rock role

A **geologist** is a scientist who studies how rocks are made, how they change, and how they make up Earth. Some geologists study geomorphology, which is how the landscape changes. This includes studying metamorphic rocks, because the age and position of metamorphic rocks are evidence of what happened to rocks in the past.

The heat from red-hot magma flowing through sedimentary rock changes the rock to metamorphic rock.

original rock unchanged

rock closest to magma changed the most

rock furthest from magma changed the least

METAMORPHIC ROCKS MADE BY PRESSURE

Some metamorphic rocks begin their journeys deep in the crust, where they are formed by enormous pressure. The changes happen over a very large area—perhaps hundreds and even thousands of miles across. This sort of **metamorphism** is called **regional metamorphism**.

Regional metamorphism happens where two **tectonic plates** are moving toward each other. One of the plates sinks under the other, and the rocks in this plate are put under huge pressure as they move down toward the **mantle**. Some change into metamorphic rocks. Others get so hot that they melt, creating lots of magma that rises into the crust. This magma heats the rocks in the plate above, creating more metamorphic rocks.

There are beautiful patterns in Lewissian gneiss found in the Western Isles of Scotland. These rocks were made by regional metamorphism.

METAMORPHIC ROCKS AND MOUNTAINS

Some of the world's great mountain ranges, such as the Alps and the Himalayas, were formed when two plates crashed slowly together. In the crust under the mountains, huge pressure created metamorphic rocks. There are often huge amounts of metamorphic rocks under mountain ranges.

Number crunching

All of the world's oldest rocks are metamorphic rocks. The oldest rock found so far is a type of schist called greenstone, found in northern Canada, which is 4.3 billion years old. Earth itself is 4.5 billion years old. See page 25 to find out how geologists measure the age of rocks.

This is some of the oldest rock on Earth. It was found near the Acasta River, in Canada.

WHAT TYPES OF METAMORPHIC ROCK ARE THERE?

There are dozens of different metamorphic rocks. How a metamorphic rock looks depends on the original rock from which it was formed, and also the place where it was made. For example, shale (a **sedimentary rock**) can be turned into the metamorphic rocks slate, **schist**, or **gneiss**.

The following are some examples of metamorphic rocks:

Slate is a dark, fine-**grained** rock made when shale is put under high pressure. It splits easily into thin sheets.

Schists are medium-grained metamorphic rocks made from shale or mudstone. There are many types of schists in different colors.

Gneiss is formed at very high temperatures and pressures from different **igneous** and sedimentary rocks. It is coarse-grained and has bands of **minerals** that are often bent and folded.

Marble is formed when **limestone** is heated to very high temperatures (see page 20).

Quartzite is formed when sandstone is heated. It is mostly made from the mineral **quartz**.

This metamorphic mica schist formation is in the Namib Desert, in Africa.

Identifying metamorphic rocks

Metamorphic rocks are normally very hard, dull in appearance, and quite rough to touch. A rock with bands of color is probably gneiss. Rocks with large **crystals** in a fine-grained background are probably metamorphic, too. You can use the table here to help you identify metamorphic rock.

Rock	Color	Foliated*	Grain size
slate	dark gray	yes	fine
schist	mixture	no	medium
gneiss	pink/gray	yes	coarse
marble	light	no	coarse
quartzite	light	no	coarse

** **Foliated** means a rock has bands of minerals in it.*

This is quartzite, a metamorphic rock made when sandstone is changed by heat and pressure. This example is in Kimberley, in Australia.

HOW DO WE USE METAMORPHIC ROCKS?

Metamorphic rocks are not commonly found on Earth's surface. Most of the rocks we use as materials are **sedimentary** and **igneous** rocks, which are easier to find. However, where metamorphic rocks are found, we use them for building and other jobs.

Schist and **gneiss** are tough rocks that are good for building. They are also crushed into gravel for making concrete and for paving. Some schists and gneisses have attractive **crystals** and patterns and are often used for decorative buildings and ornamental stonework.

Slate has some very useful properties. It can be easily split into flat sheets, and it is almost completely waterproof. This makes it a popular material for making roof and floor tiles. Monuments and nameplates are also made from slate because it is easy to carve.

These traditional houses in Nepal have roofs made from slate, a metamorphic rock, split into thin sheets.

18

METAMORPHIC ROCKS IN THE PAST

Rocks were one of the first materials that humans used. We do not know when people first used metamorphic rocks, but it may have been hundreds of thousands of years ago—possibly to make simple tools, or shelters.

Rock role

A sculptor is a craftsperson who shapes materials to make statues and other sculptures. The sculptor uses tools such as chisels to cut away the rock. Sculptors often work with rock because it will last for a long time. Schists, gneisses, slates, and **marbles** are all used for sculpture.

These standing stones were erected thousands of years ago at Callanish, on the island of Lewis in Scotland. They are made of Lewissian gneiss.

MARVELOUS MARBLE

Marble is a metamorphic rock that is formed when **limestone** is changed by high temperatures. It is made mostly from a **mineral** called **calcite** (also called calcium carbonate). Pure marble is mostly white, but marble often contains other minerals that create colors, such as black, red, and green, and beautiful patterns.

Marble is quite easy to cut and polish to make a shiny finish. That is why marble is used for decoration in buildings. It can be found on the outside of buildings and on walls and floors. Marble is also used for making ornaments and sculptures. Some other decorative rocks look like marble and are sometimes called marble, but they are not actually metamorphic rock.

This sample of Balkan Gray marble has beautiful gray and pink patterns. The white lines are called veins.

The calcite that becomes marble is an important raw material in industry. It is used in making things from paper to toothpaste. Lime, a material used to make cement, is made by heating calcite.

Rock role

Marble is found all over the world, and marble with different colors and patterns comes from different areas. The most famous marble comes from around the city of Carrara in Italy. White and gray marble from Carrara have been used by builders and sculptors for hundreds of years.

The famous statue of the biblical hero David by the Italian artist Michelangelo is carved from Carrara marble.

DO METAMORPHIC ROCKS LAST FOREVER?

How long do metamorphic rocks last before their journey ends? It is normally a very, very long time! A metamorphic rock such as a **gneiss**, made many miles down in Earth's **crust**, will last for many millions of years. Some metamorphic rocks are billions of years old. But metamorphic rocks do not last forever. Their journey eventually comes to an end.

DESTRUCTION AT EARTH'S SURFACE

Sometimes metamorphic rocks that are made deep in the crust end up at Earth's surface. Then the rocks are worn away by processes called **weathering** and **erosion**.

The jagged peaks of the Mont Blanc range in the French Alps show how ice breaks up solid rock.

Weathering is the way rocks are broken up by the action of weather. For example, in very cold places, water freezes inside cracks in the rocks and helps to break them up. Flowing water, wind, and gravity carry the broken pieces of rock away.

Flowing water and glaciers (huge masses of ice that travel down valleys) also break up the rocks they flow over. But metamorphic rocks are tough, and they wear away very slowly.

Science tip

On a trip to coastal areas, or to hills or mountains, you can see how rocks are worn away. At coastal areas, look for how cliffs are broken up by the waves—there will be broken rocks around their bases. Near hills and mountains, look for loose and broken rocks and see how the broken pieces are carried downhill by streams.

The regular movement of ocean waves causes erosion at the base of sea cliffs.

23

DESTRUCTION UNDERGROUND

Metamorphic rocks are destroyed where two **tectonic plates** are moving toward each other. If part of the plate sinks down into the crust or comes under pressure, any metamorphic rocks inside it are heated up and melted. The **molten** rock (**magma**) from them can rise up into the crust, cool down, and so form new **igneous rocks**.

It is not just igneous and **sedimentary rocks** that are changed into metamorphic rocks. Metamorphic rocks themselves can be changed into other metamorphic rocks. For example, a rock such as a **schist** made by **regional metamorphism** could be changed into a new form of rock by **local metamorphism**.

In the distant future, this gneiss in Scotland could be turned into another sort of metamorphic rock.

MEASURING THE AGE OF ROCKS

Geologists often need to find out how old rocks are. For example, the age of a piece of schist might them tell them when an ancient mountain range was formed. The main way of dating metamorphic rock is by radiometric dating. This method relies on the fact that, over time, some types of **atoms** change into other types (a process called radioactive decay). The amount of various types of atom in a sample is measured to figure out the age.

GEOLOGICAL TIMELINE

The age of metamorphic rocks is measured in millions of years. Age is also given by the name of the period in time when it was made. For example, a Devonian rock was made between 359 and 416 million years ago.

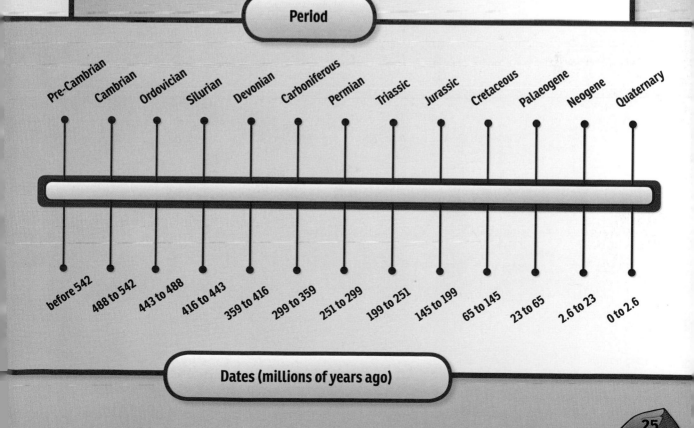

Period

Pre-Cambrian — before 542
Cambrian — 488 to 542
Ordovician — 443 to 488
Silurian — 416 to 443
Devonian — 359 to 416
Carboniferous — 299 to 359
Permian — 251 to 299
Triassic — 199 to 251
Jurassic — 145 to 199
Cretaceous — 65 to 145
Palaeogene — 23 to 65
Neogene — 2.6 to 23
Quaternary — 0 to 2.6

Dates (millions of years ago)

ARE WE HARMING METAMORPHIC ROCKS?

Metamorphic rocks such as **marble** and slate are an important resource for us. But we destroy these rocks when we take them from the ground. Rocks are dug out at **quarries**. Lots of energy is needed to dig out rocks and transport them, and digging them out creates noise and pollution. Quarrying destroys natural **habitats** for wildlife—although disused, flooded quarries often make good habitats for birds.

Rocks are destroyed and **recycled** in the **rock cycle** on a massive scale in the **crust** many miles down. Quarrying on the surface has very little effect on the rock cycle. However, we should try not to damage natural rocks, because they are part of our environment.

This disused quarry in Wales has become a river habitat for wildlife.

JOURNEY'S END

Our journey of metamorphic rock has come to its end. The journey began inside Earth's crust, where rocks were changed by extreme heat and immense pressure to make metamorphic rocks. The heat came from **molten** rock moving into the crust, and the pressure came from **tectonic plates** crushing into each other.

During the rock cycle, new metamorphic rocks are being made all the time, and old metamorphic rocks are being destroyed all the time. The rock cycle has been going on since Earth was made 4.5 billion years ago, and it will continue for billions of years to come.

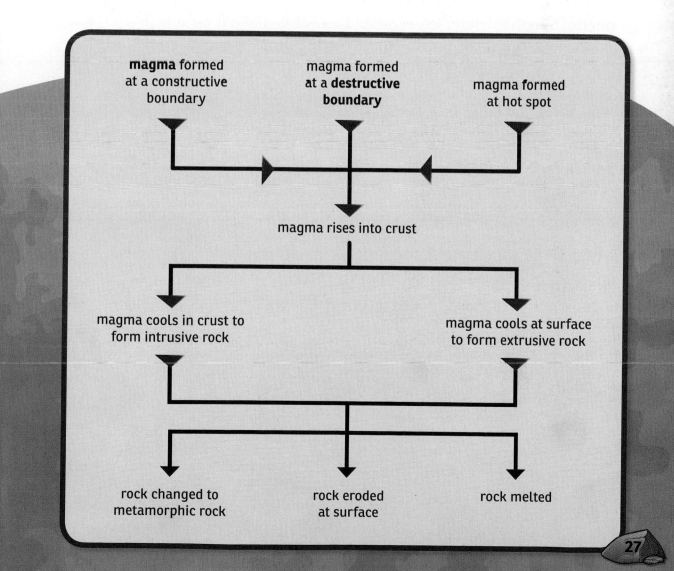

MAKE CLAY AND CHOCOLATE ROCKS!

Here's a simple experiment that will help you to understand the journey of metamorphic rocks that we have followed through this book. Before you try the experiment, read the instructions, prepare the materials you need, and find an area where you can work.

Ask an adult to help you with this experiment.

YOU WILL NEED:

- modeling clay
- chocolate
- aluminum foil
- a heavy book
- a plate
- a knife
- a microwave oven.

WHAT TO DO:

1. Break the chocolate into small pieces less than 1 centimeter (half an inch) across.

2. Take a lump of modeling clay about 6–7 centimeters (2–3 inches) across. Push the chocolate pieces into it and roll it into a ball.

3. Put the ball on the plate and put it into a microwave oven. Warm it on low power for about two minutes.

4. Put a piece of aluminum foil over the ball and put a heavy book on top of the foil. Wait for a few minutes.

5 Cut the crushed ball in half—carefully, since it might still be hot.

What do you see inside the ball? Did you get layered patterns? The heat and pressure you applied changed the structure of the clay and chocolate mixture, just as heat and pressure change **sedimentary** and **igneous rocks** into metamorphic rocks.

GLOSSARY

atom smallest particle of chemical matter that can exist

calcite type of mineral found in limestone rock

collision boundary boundary where two tectonic plates come together, creating immense pressure

continent one of the large landmasses of Earth, such as Europe, Africa, or Asia

core central part of Earth

crust rocky surface layer of Earth

crystal shape a mineral grows into as a result of the neat rows and columns of atoms

destructive boundary boundary between two tectonic plates where rocks in the plates are destroyed

erosion wearing away of rocks by flowing water, wind, and glaciers

geologist scientist who studies the rocks and soil from which Earth is made

gneiss common coarse-grained metamorphic rock

grain pattern of particles in a rock (the particles can be crystals or small pieces of rock)

granite common intrusive igneous rock

habitat place where an animal or plant lives

igneous rock rock formed when magma (molten rock) cools and solidifies

limestone common sedimentary rock made up of the mineral calcite, which can come from the shells and skeletons of sea animals

local metamorphism when metamorphic rocks are made over a small area (up to a few miles across), normally by contact with hot magma

magma molten rock below Earth's crust

mantle very deep layer of hot rock below Earth's crust

marble metamorphic rock made from the sedimentary rock limestone

metamorphism change that happens when rock becomes metamorphic rock

mineral substance that is naturally present in Earth, such as gold and salt

molten melted

particle small piece of material

plate boundary place where one tectonic plate meets another

pressure force or weight pressing against something

quarry place where large amounts of rock are dug out of the ground

quartz hard mineral, often found in crystal form

recycle process of changing something into something new

regional metamorphism when metamorphic rocks are made over a large area (perhaps hundreds or even thousands of miles across), normally by pressure in the crust

rock cycle constant formation, destruction, and recycling of rocks through Earth's crust

schist common medium-grained metamorphic rock

sedimentary rock rock made when tiny pieces of rock or the skeletons or shells of sea animals are buried underground and compressed

tectonic plate one of the giant pieces that Earth's crust is cracked into

volcano opening in Earth's surface where magma escapes from underground

weathering breaking up of rocks by weather conditions such as extremes of temperature

FIND OUT MORE

BOOKS

Faulkner, Rebecca. *Metamorphic Rock* (Geology Rocks!). Chicago: Raintree, 2008.

Pipe, Jim. *Earth's Rocks and Fossils* (Planet Earth). Pleasantville, N.Y.: Gareth Stevens, 2008.

Walker, Sally M. *Rocks* (Early Bird Earth Science). Minneapolis: Lerner, 2007.

WEBSITES

See animations of how rocks are formed at this website of the Franklin Institute: **www.fi.edu/fellows/fellow1/oct98/create**

Find lots of information about rocks and minerals, as well as links to other interesting websites, at this site: **www.rocksforkids.com**

PLACES TO VISIT

American Museum of Natural History
Central Park West at 79th Street
New York, New York, 10024-5192
Tel: (212) 769-5100
www.amnh.org
Visit a large and fascinating collection of rocks, minerals, and fossils.

The Field Museum
1400 S. Lake Shore Drive
Chicago, Illinois 60605-2496
Tel: (312) 922-9410
www.fieldmuseum.org
See fascinating exhibits of rocks, minerals, and fossils from around the world.

INDEX

EMERGENCY WORKERS

HAZMAT

by
Jim Ollhoff

VISIT US AT:
WWW.ABDOPUBLISHING.COM

Published by ABDO Publishing Company, PO Box 398166, Minneapolis, MN 55439.
Copyright ©2013 by Abdo Consulting Group, Inc. International copyrights reserved
in all countries. No part of this book may be reproduced in any form without written
permission from the publisher. ABDO & Daughters™ is a trademark and logo of
ABDO Publishing Company.

Printed in the United States of America, North Mankato, Minnesota.
052012
092012

♻ PRINTED ON RECYCLED PAPER

Editor: John Hamilton
Graphic Design: Sue Hamilton
Cover Design: Neil Klinepier
Cover Photo: iStockphoto
Interior Photos and Illustrations: Alaska Dept of Environmental Conservation-pg 21;
AP-pgs 18-19 & 20; Corbis-pgs 13, 23 & 24; Getty Images-pgs 22 & 25; Glow Images-pgs 1,
5 & 29; iStockphoto-pgs 14-15, 27 & 32; Thinkstock-pgs 6-12, 16-18, 20, 22, 26, & 30;
United States Customs & Border Protection-pg 3.

ABDO Booklinks
To learn more about Emergency Workers, visit ABDO Publishing Company online. Web
sites about Emergency Workers are featured on our Book Links pages. These links are
routinely monitored and updated to provide the most current information available. Web
site: www.abdopublishing.com

Library of Congress Cataloging-in-Publication Data

Hazmat / Jim Ollhoff.
   p. cm. -- (Emergency workers)
 Includes index.
 ISBN 978-1-61783-514-8
 1. Hazardous substances--Juvenile literature. 2. Hazardous waste site remediation-
-Juvenile literature. 3. Hazardous waste management industry--Juvenile literature.
4. Pollution control industry--Juvenile literature. 5. Hazardous occupations--Juvenile
literature.
 T55.3.H3H447 2013
 363.17'8--dc23
                                    2012009609

TABLE OF CONTENTS

THE HAZMAT TECHNICIAN

A pickup truck crashes. Its cargo includes chemicals that are used to clean swimming pools. Hundreds of gallons of acid spill onto the roadway. Traffic backs up for miles, and several people who inhaled toxic fumes have to be taken to the hospital.

A tanker ship traveling downriver runs aground. Its hull ruptures. Its cargo is a solvent, a chemical that causes other chemicals to dissolve. Homes downstream must be evacuated.

An underground storage tank is full of benzene, a chemical used to make plastics. Over time, the tank has corroded, and the benzene gas begins to leak. People downwind begin to complain of dizziness, headaches, and uncontrollable shaking. Some people have fallen unconscious.

All of these events are spills of hazardous materials. Hazmats can be liquid, gas, or solid. Liquids might float or mix in streams or rivers, or spread across surface areas. Gases can be carried by the wind. Solids can cause explosions or catch fire. Hazmats are dangerous to people and the environment.

When hazardous materials enter the environment, hazmat technicians are called in to handle the situation. They must figure out what the hazardous material is, what the risk is, and how to clean it up.

WHAT ARE HAZMATS?

A hazardous material, or hazmat, is anything that poses a health risk to people or a risk to the environment. In fact, there are many hazardous materials in the average home. Bug sprays or oven cleaners can make people sick if they are inhaled. Drain cleaners can irritate or damage skin, and are poisonous if swallowed. Glass cleaners can irritate eyes. Motor oil and paint must be disposed of in special ways because they can cause environmental damage if they are dumped on the ground or in the water.

Some hazardous materials simply irritate the skin. Others are labeled "caustic" or "corrosive," which means they work like an acid. They can severely damage skin or other materials. Some hazmats are flammable. Others are very dangerous to plants and animals. Many hazmats are poisonous to people.

We need hazardous materials. They heat our homes, and they power our cars. Hazardous materials are used to create medicines. They help clean our swimming pools, our homes, and the factories where food is made. Creative scientists are needed to invent materials that are not hazardous. But until then, we continue to use dangerous and hazardous materials.

FUNGICIDES
INSECTICIDES
DANGER
KEEP OUT

Hazardous materials are used every day. Cautious, careful usage are important to keep people from becoming sick.

NINE CLASSES OF HAZMATS

The United States Department of Transportation oversees more than three billion tons (2.7 billion metric tons) of hazmats each year. These materials are shipped over highways, by airplanes, and across the water. The Department of Transportation has divided hazardous materials into nine different types, or classes.

1. EXPLOSIVES

This is any kind of material that can explode. The blast might be big or small. It might cause a fire, or the blast might shoot out objects. Examples of materials in this class include dynamite, fireworks, or ammunition.

2. GASES

Some gases are compressed, which means they are under great pressure. These gases can be dangerous if not handled carefully. Some gases are flammable, such as hydrogen. Some gases are poisonous when inhaled, such as chlorine or fluorine.

3. FLAMMABLE LIQUIDS

These are liquids that can easily catch fire. An example of this class includes gasoline. A small flame or spark can quickly set gasoline ablaze. Some flammable liquids need to be kept at a certain temperature, or they can become unstable and risk exploding into flame.

4. FLAMMABLE SOLIDS

These are materials that are solid, but can burst into flame. For example, the material on the head of a match is called phosphorus. If it is not handled carefully, it can start on fire. Some substances, when wet, will produce a flammable gas.

5. OXIDIZING AGENTS AND ORGANIC PEROXIDES

These are substances that make a chemical reaction. They often release oxygen, or some other gas. When there is too much oxygen in one place, it can make a fire burn faster and hotter.

6. TOXINS AND INFECTIOUS SUBSTANCES

Toxins are poisonous to people, and can cause harm or even death. Pesticides are in this class. An infectious substance is anything that can get people sick. This includes used hospital needles, or cultures of viruses or dangerous bacteria.

7. RADIOACTIVE MATERIALS

These are substances that emit radiation, such as uranium or plutonium.

8. CORROSIVES

A corrosive works like an acid. It can burn or destroy human flesh, and sometimes eat through certain kinds of metals or plastics. Examples of corrosives include sulfuric acid or hydrochloric acid.

9. MISCELLANEOUS

This class is for anything that is dangerous to humans or the environment, but doesn't fit into any other category. Asbestos is one example. It was used for many years in building materials, but was later found to cause cancer.

WHAT IS A HAZMAT TECHNICIAN?

Hazmat technicians are people who help when a toxic material is spilled. When there is an accident involving hazardous materials, hazmat technicians are called in. They identify what was spilled, and work to contain it. They help rescue the injured, and figure out how to fix whatever went wrong. They work to decontaminate the area to make it safe again.

There are between 15,000 and 20,000 hazmat spills every year in the United States. Most of these occur on highways, involving accidents with big trucks that spill toxic cargo.

Because hazmat spills are not very common in any one area, most hazmat technicians also have other jobs. Many firefighters are trained as hazmat technicians. Police officers, Emergency Medical Technicians (EMTs), and hospital nurses are often trained as hazmat technicians as well.

New York City police officers in hazmat suits work at the site of a steam pipe explosion. The violent eruption threw asbestos-tainted debris into the air and had to be cleaned up to make the area safe.

Hazmat technicians work as a team to safely dispose of dangerous chemicals.

Hazmat technicians have to be good team players. There are many different roles within a hazmat team. Some do research—what has spilled and what will the effects be? Some have to figure out how to work with police to close off a dangerous area, or work with firefighters if there is fire. There is often a decontamination team. They work to remove hazardous materials from people who have been exposed. Every hazmat spill is different. Everyone has to work

together to determine and execute the correct response. Rescuing people is always the first priority. After that, hazmat technicians work together to save the environment and property.

Hazmat technicians always need to continue their training. New materials are being introduced all the time. Which ones are toxic? If there is a spill, how can it be decontaminated? Hazmat technicians always have to be up to date.

CALM, COOL, AND COLLECTED

Hazmat technicians must remain calm, cool, and collected in dangerous situations. They can't panic or get scared and run away. Their decisions can affect people for years to come.

When hazmat technicians arrive at an accident scene, they try to enter the area upwind, so the wind doesn't blow any toxins directly at them. If there are people present who have already suffered injuries or are contaminated, they get them safely to assistance. Getting people to safety is always the most important job.

Determining what substance has been spilled is crucial. Hazmat technicians need to know the effects of the chemical on people and the environment, and what might happen if it mixes with other substances in the area. They work with police to evacuate people when necessary. They must be excellent communicators to ensure everyone has good information during an emergency.

If a chemical is actively spilling or leaking, hazmat technicians have to figure out how to stop it. They need to understand how to shut off valves or put patches on broken seals. Sometimes, there is no ready-made patch, and they have to be creative to stop a leak.

Finally, hazmat technicians need to stop spills from being dangerous. This is called "neutralizing the spill." It may require adding chemicals or other materials. They need to decontaminate themselves and others, which often means getting doused with huge amounts of water.

Hazmat technicians sometimes clean up a spill and declare the area safe. But emergency response hazmat teams usually aren't involved in long-term clean up. Organizations hire special teams to come in and cleanup, because they may have to be there for a long time.

A hazmat technician is decontaminated using huge amounts of water and detergent blasted through a water spray unit. The water is then collected and disposed of safely.

TRAINING

There are many different ways to get hazmat training. Some courses are offered by colleges. Some are offered by other organizations. Sometimes training is online. Other times it happens in a classroom or lab. Usually, training includes a combination of computer simulations and real-world situations.

Different states have different requirements for training. Training also depends on a person's specific job within the hazmat team. Some hazmat technicians might spend 40 hours in training, others might spend 400 hours. Most programs require continuing education every year or every few years.

Some hazmat technicians specialize in railroad cars. Others are chemical specialists. Some are biological specialists or radiation specialists. Some technicians receive specialized training in how to clean up areas that have been contaminated by illegal drugs.

A hazmat professional brings out evidence from a home police believe was used as an illegal drug manufacturing lab.

Most types of training cover the basics of chemical hazardous materials, including their identification and how they react with other substances. Students learn how to predict what the risks will be, and how to decontaminate people who have been exposed. They learn how to neutralize or clean up dangerous spills. Finally, they learn how to create emergency plans for what to do in a crisis.

THE HAZMAT SUIT

Hazmat technicians work in very dangerous situations, often with poisonous chemicals or gases. They often wear special gear to protect themselves. Protective suits are categorized from Level A to Level D, based on how much protection they provide.

Level A protection is a suit that totally covers the technician from head to toe. Most liquids and gases cannot penetrate the Level A suit. Hazmat technicians still have to be careful to avoid anything that might puncture the suit, or acids that might eat a hole through it. A two-way communication radio and a breathing apparatus are included inside the suit. The breathing apparatus holds a limited amount of air, so the suit can't be worn indefinitely. It can be difficult to move in a Level A suit, and it gets hot inside quickly.

The amount of time that a person can wear a Level A suit is limited.

An Alaska hazmat team wears Level B suits during a cleanup mission.

Level B protection is also head-to-toe, but is not airtight. It is worn when there is danger from hazardous liquids, but not from gas. The breathing apparatus may be worn outside the suit.

Level C protection is what a firefighter might wear. Level C suits are sometimes called splash suits. They may use a breathing apparatus. These suits protect technicians from splashing water or chemicals, often when they are decontaminating the Level A or Level B technicians.

Level D protection is not really a suit at all. This level refers to normal clothes worn by people working in the environment. It may include coveralls, boots, gloves, and safety goggles.

CLEANING UP NUCLEAR DISASTERS

In March 2011, an earthquake and tsunami hit Japan with terrible force. The tsunami knocked out the cooling system of the Fukushima Daiichi nuclear power plant. Without the ability to cool, the nuclear material overheated and melted, releasing dangerous radioactivity into the air and water. Radioactive particles, blown by the wind, were detected as far away as the United States and Canada. Experts say it will be decades before the Fukushima Daiichi plant can be fully decontaminated.

Technicians work in hazmat suits in the control room of the Fukushima Daiichi plant just weeks after the March 2011 disaster.

Workers bury Chernobyl's damaged Reactor 4 in 1986. The Chernobyl power plant meltdown was the worst nuclear disaster in history. The area is still radioactive today.

Radioactivity and radioactive particles are an especially disturbing hazardous material. Radiation can last a long time. The worst nuclear accident was a 1986 meltdown in the Chernobyl nuclear power plant in Ukraine. Even today, there is a vast area around the plant that is not safe for people.

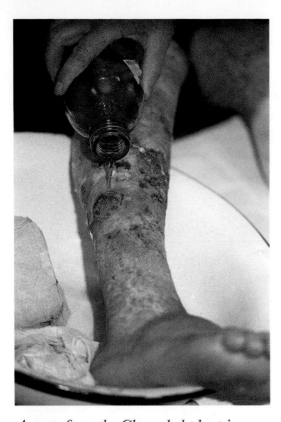

A man from the Chernobyl plant is treated for radiation burns on his leg.

Radiation can cause burns. It can cause people to become very sick, and their hair can fall out. Radiation can damage the body's DNA, causing cancer. Intense radiation can cause death in a short time.

When hazmat technicians respond to radiation emergencies, they must wear protective equipment. They may wear a radiation dosimeter, which tells them how much radiation is present on their body. They may carry a Geiger counter, which tells them which objects are radioactive and which are not. Technicians can also use the Geiger counter to discover if people have been contaminated with radioactive particles.

Victims who are exposed to radioactive particles need to be doused with lots of water. This washes away the radioactive particles, although in some cases, the damage is already done.

Radioactive material sometimes is simply buried in the ground, or mixed with cement. Robots can sometimes help sweep up radioactive particles. However, if they spend too much time doing this activity, the robots themselves become radioactive and must be buried also.

Hazmat technicians, whether dealing with radiation leaks or chemical spills, must take care of themselves and other people. They must be brave as well as calm, working to rescue people in the worst emergencies.

Nuclear research lab technicians test an area for radiation using a Geiger counter.

INTERVIEW WITH A HAZMAT TECHNICIAN

Chuck Solseth started his firefighter and hazmat training in Cedar Rapids, Iowa, in 1991. He is currently a battalion chief for the Rochester, Minnesota, fire department, where he also served as the hazmat team coordinator. He was asked to be Rochester's representative to the state of Minnesota's multi-agency hazmat response team. He worked at the hazmat station in Rochester for 10 years before taking a position as training captain, and still assists with hazmat training.

Q: How did you get interested in being a hazmat technician?

Solseth: When I was a new firefighter, I went on a few hazmat calls. During these calls I realized how little I knew about hazmat response. Not knowing what you are doing greatly increases the chance of hurting yourself and possibly others. I wanted to know what I was doing, so I started attending classes.

Q: What is an average day like as a hazmat technician?

Solseth: I'm a hazmat technician, but I'm also a firefighter and have EMS (Emergency Medical Services) duties with the fire department. Between calls and fire and EMS training, I have to keep the hazmat equipment in good working order. Maintenance includes monitor calibrations, chemical suit tests, and equipment repairs. I also have to train with the equipment to maintain proficiency. Practice chemical suit entries, computer modeling of a chemical spill, and patching and plugging exercises are some of the training we do. Just knowing where all the equipment is stored on the hazmat rig is a daunting task for any firefighter.

Q: What's your most memorable experience as a hazmat technician?

Solseth: My first entry was probably the most memorable. I had to secure an ammonia leak at a manufacturing plant. I went in with a captain and located a remote valve that we secured to stop the leak. We approached from the upwind side in our big blue responder suits and stopped that leak! I was hooked after that. I stood a little taller that day among some pretty experienced and seasoned firefighters.

Q: What's the best part about being a hazmat technician?

Solseth: It is an elite team. You have to be smart and technically savvy. It separates me from the other firefighters and makes me valuable to my department and the community I serve. It is important for me to be involved, and the more training I receive, the more opportunities I have to make a difference in my community.

Q: What advice would you have for someone who wants to be a hazmat technician?

Solseth: Listen in your chemistry classes. It is hard to believe, but I use the principals of chemistry I learned from my chemistry teacher in seventh grade. The combustible gas experiments and the vapor density experiments he taught me I use almost every day. I wish I had paid more attention those days. I never thought I would be protecting lives as a hazmat technician.

Firefighters in hazmat gear train to handle a toxic spill accident. They learn what to do to help the victims, as well as clean up the spill.

GLOSSARY

ASBESTOS

A heat-resistant mineral used in making insulating and fire-resistant materials. Once used in building insulation, asbestos was found to cause certain cancers. It is no longer used, but is still found in older buildings. It must be removed and disposed of by hazmat professionals.

CONTAMINATION

When an uncontrolled hazardous substance affects people or the environment.

CORROSIVE

A substance that works like an acid. It can burn or destroy human flesh, and sometimes eat through certain kinds of metals or plastics.

DECONTAMINATE

Making an area safe for people after a spill of hazardous material. Also making people, such as hazmat technicians, firefighters, and police officers, safe after working in a contaminated area.

DNA

DNA is short for the scientific term deoxyribonucleic acid. In living things, DNA is the material inside the center of every cell that forms genes. This material is inherited from an individual's parents.

EMERGENCY MEDICAL SERVICES (EMS)

An organized group of services, including 911 emergency call centers and trained EMTs and paramedics, that helps people in emergency situations get to a hospital for care.

EVACUATE

To leave a dangerous place to go to a place of safety.

FLAMMABLE

Something that is easily set on fire, such as gasoline.

GEIGER COUNTER

A device that measures the amount of radioactive contamination on people or objects.

HAZMAT (HAZARDOUS MATERIAL)

Any substance that can cause harm to people, the environment, or property.

RADIOACTIVITY

A stream of particles that emits from a source such as uranium. This energy can cause sickness or be fatal to people who are exposed to the radiation.

TOXIN

Something that causes living things to sicken and sometimes die.

INDEX